THEN & NOW

MOUNTAIN VIEW

OPPOSITE: Horse-drawn buggies line the sidewalk of an unpaved Castro Street in this 1904 photograph taken from Front Street (now Evelyn Avenue). Although decades of modernization have changed this scene a great deal, downtown Mountain View is fortunate to retain some landmarks that bear witness to the city's rich history. One example is the Weilheimer Building, identifiable on the right by its large "General Merchandise" sign. Built in 1870, the structure is a rare example of architecture from Mountain View's earliest decades. (Courtesy Mountain View Historical Association.)

THEN & NOW

MOUNTAIN VIEW

Nicholas Perry
Photographs by Kimberly Chan

This book is dedicated to Mountain View city historian Barbara McPheeters Kinchen in gratitude for her assistance on this project and in honor of all she has done to record and preserve Mountain View's history for future generations.

Copyright © 2012 by Nicholas Perry
ISBN 978-0-7385-9576-4

Library of Congress Control Number: 2012934929

Published by Arcadia Publishing
Charleston, South Carolina

Printed in the United States of America

Then and Now is a registered trademark and is used under license from Salamander Books Limited

For all general information, please contact Arcadia Publishing:
Telephone 843-853-2070
Fax 843-853-0044
E-mail sales@arcadiapublishing.com
For customer service and orders:
Toll-Free 1-888-313-2665

Visit us on the Internet at www.arcadiapublishing.com

ON THE FRONT COVER: Buildings from nearly every decade of Mountain View's history stand along Castro Street. The northeast corner of Castro and Villa Streets illustrates this architectural legacy. The 1904 image features the McDonald & Burke Blacksmith on the corner. The blacksmith was replaced in 1906 by the Mockbee Building, which still stands today. In the center stands the Ames Building, built in 1903 and restored in 2003. (Historical image courtesy Mountain View Historical Association, contemporary photograph by Nicholas Perry.)

ON THE BACK COVER: Many prominent Mountain View landmarks exist today only in photographs and memories. However, one lost civic landmark, Mountain View's 1888 Southern Pacific train depot, has risen from the past. This photograph shows the historic depot shortly before it was demolished in 1959 and replaced by a simple concrete shelter. In 2002, to celebrate Mountain View's 100th year of incorporation, a replica of the depot was built in the city's Centennial Plaza. (Courtesy Mountain View Historical Association.)

CONTENTS

ACKNOWLEDGMENTS

Writing Then & Now: *Mountain View* was a pleasure thanks to the assistance of many individuals and organizations. The Mountain View Historical Association (MVHA) supplied most of this book's "then" images. Many members also offered images: Peggy Crowder, Cliff Del Carlo, Kevin Duggan, Patricia Diaz, Wallace and Ruth Erichsen, Katherine Gemello, Edna Pear, Matt Pear, Carol Rudgers, Eugene Sharp, and Honor Spitz. Thank you, I wish I could include all of your photographs!

The second major source of historical images was the Mountain View Public Library (MVPL). Bill Stubkjaer at the Moffett Field Historical Society, Carol Patane at St. Francis High School, Corine Bernard at Villa Siena, and Jim Hickman also provided photographs and assistance. The Mountain View History Center archives, Mary Jo Ignoffo's *Milestones: A History of Mountain View*, and Mountain View's 2008 Historic Resource Survey by Carey & Co., Inc., were informative resources.

A huge thanks to Kimberly Chan (www.kimberlychanphotography.com) for providing the majority of the book's "now" photographs. To simplify credits, "now" photographs on pages 33, 44, 48, 56, 58, 66, 72, 79, 82, 85, 87–91, and 94–95 were taken by me; all other "now" photographs are by Kimberly Chan. Kimberly and I jointly thank her husband and my good friend, Matthew Chan, along with our mutual friends for their support.

My editor Amy Perryman and the rest of the team at Arcadia Publishing provided helpful assistance from afar. I also benefited from a fantastic local editing team of friends and family; Barbara Kinchen, Joe Peltier, Preeti Piplani, my aunt Elise Sias, my brother Chris, and my parents Mark and Gloria all helped shape this book's content. Extra special thanks to Joe; not only was he an unofficial editor extraordinaire, his support and encouragement during every phase of this project was simply awesome. I would also like to acknowledge my wonderful grandmothers, Emma Sias and Elizabeth Perry, who have connected me to the rich history of this region, as did my late grandfather, Simon Sias, who will forever remain one of my greatest heroes. Thank you to all my other family members, friends, and coworkers for your encouragement.

Finally, thanks to all the readers of this book for taking the time to discover Mountain View's history. For those who have known Mountain View for many years, I hope this book brings back fond memories and offers new insights into familiar places. For those newer to the area, I hope each "then and now" comparison offers an interesting glimpse into Mountain View's past.

INTRODUCTION

A "then and now" photographic history of Mountain View is perhaps one of the best ways to explore this dynamic city's evolution. From one end of town to the other, hidden stories of the city's development can be uncovered by comparing and contrasting what was with what is. Rather than attempting to summarize Mountain View's entire history, this introduction seeks to set the stage for this journey into the past by focusing only on the major milestones that have shaped the city's modern landscape.

Mountain View lies between the foothills of the Santa Cruz Mountains and the marshy shores of the southern San Francisco Bay. The fertile land between these two geographic features once supported multiple villages of the native Ohlone people. During the Spanish era, missionaries utilized the land for sheep pastures. This use inspired the name of Rancho Pastoría de las Borregas (Ranch of the Ewe/ Lamb Pasture), an 8,800-acre land grant bestowed to Francisco Estrada by the Mexican government in 1842. In 1845, the rancho was transferred to Mariano Castro. Typical of the oldest sites featured in this book, photographs of Castro's 1850 adobe contrast sharply with the Central Expressway strip mall located there today.

Mountain View's origins as a distinct community began during the Gold Rush. El Camino Real's crossing at Stevens Creek was a convenient resting place for stagecoaches traveling between San Jose and San Francisco. In 1852, a stagecoach stop was established, and as the decade progressed, a small settlement formed around the stop. Local lore attributes the town's name to its first postmaster, Jacob Shumway, who was inspired by the clear view of the surrounding coastal mountain ranges. The stretch of El Camino Real between Calderon Avenue and Stevens Creek became the main street of the small town.

When the railroad was built in 1864, it bypassed Mountain View, curtailing the original town's growth. A train depot one mile to the north spurred development of today's downtown along Castro Street. This new settlement was known as Mountain View Station or New Mountain View, and the original town became known as Old Mountain View. When Mountain View officially incorporated on November 7, 1902, Old Mountain View remained just outside the city limits. Over time, the two towns merged. Buildings from the original town survived as reminders of its presence until the 1950s. In a confusing twist of history, the area once known as New Mountain View is now commonly referred to as Old Mountain View.

Mountain View grew at a relatively steady pace during the first half of the 20th century. A notable growth spurt occurred in 1904, when the Seventh-Day Adventist–owned Pacific Press Publishing Association relocated from Oakland. About 100 Adventist families settled the neighborhood south of the press's Villa Street campus. By the late 1920s, Mountain View's developed area roughly encompassed a rectangle bounded by Chiquita Avenue on the west, Jackson Street on the north, Calderon Avenue on the east, and El Camino Real on the south. These boundaries remained largely unchanged until the 1950s.

The highly productive agricultural lands surrounding Mountain View during its first century helped earn the Santa Clara Valley its nickname, the Valley of Heart's Delight. Seemingly endless orchards stretched south of the city, and to the north, a patchwork of orchards, farms, nurseries, and dairies extended to the San Francisco Bay's wetlands.

A few small clusters of development existed in the countryside, including the Junction and University Park. The Junction emerged in the early 1900s as a concentration of businesses at the intersection of El Camino Real and El Monte Road. The 1908 University Park subdivision near the Castro family's railroad station on Pastoria Avenue (now Rengstorff Avenue) was meant to become a country suburb for Stanford University professors and San Franciscans. But by the 1950s, it was known as Castro City, a working-class Latino neighborhood.

As Mountain View slowly grew, people of varied backgrounds moved to the city to partake in its commercial and agricultural prosperity. The town developed into an ethnically diverse blue-collar city that stood in contrast to its more suburban neighbors on the peninsula. By the 1920s, distinct ethnic neighborhoods existed within the city—Spanish-speaking residents concentrated north of the railroad tracks, and the Asian community centered near the intersection of Villa and View Streets, an area once known as Mountain View's Chinatown.

The establishment of Moffett Field in 1933 did not spur much physical expansion of Mountain View but definitely helped the city weather the Great Depression. Moffett Boulevard was built as an extension of Castro Street and directly linked Mountain View with the Navy's new airfield. The boulevard was a strategic move by the city to connect the base to Mountain View rather than to neighboring Sunnyvale. Over time, a few motels, bars, and restaurants concentrated just outside Moffett Field's main gate on the old Bayshore Highway (Highway 101).

California's post–World War II population boom fueled an era of phenomenal growth in Mountain View. Between 1950 and 1960, the city's population ballooned from 6,563 to 30,889. The countryside north of El Camino Real and south of the Bayshore Highway rapidly gave way to a mix of apartments, single-family homes, and industrial parks. Simultaneously, the vast orchard district south of El Camino Real developed almost exclusively into single-family-home subdivisions. The incorporation of the City of Los Altos in 1952 initiated an annexation war over orchard land that resulted in today's zigzagging city limits.

Whisman Road, near the city's eastern edge, became one of Silicon Valley's earliest high-tech industrial districts. San Antonio Road, near the city's western edge, became a new suburban commercial center for the region. As downtown Castro Street struggled, El Camino Real reemerged as the city's premier commercial thoroughfare, lined with postwar commercial landmarks.

The rural area north of Highway 101, known today as the North Bayshore, was the last portion of Mountain View to be urbanized. It was first settled in the 1850s, when early pioneers like Henry Rengstorff established ship landings along the San Francisco Bay. South of these marshy shores, an agricultural district and rural residential area emerged. By the 1970s, the North Bayshore was home to a hodgepodge of farms, dumps, and even the testing ground for early Disneyland rides. The 1990s dot-com boom erased the last vestiges of the district's rural past, and today the area is home to campuses of world-renowned high-tech companies. Over 750 acres of open space and converted landfill along the city's bay frontage was preserved as Shoreline Regional Park and Wildlife Refuge.

The development of Mountain View's last rural area ushered in an era of redevelopment that continues to this day. Early industrial parks and underutilized commercial strips are now being transformed into new neighborhoods. Prewar areas like Castro Street and the surrounding historic residential neighborhoods have been given new life and vibrancy. Even venerable old El Camino Real is slowly being transformed into a grand boulevard as mixed-use buildings replace strip malls, giving the historic highway a new sense of urbanity. As the city continues to redevelop, many of the "now" photographs featured in this book may quickly become interesting "then" photographs over the coming years. Hopefully, through sustained stewardship of its most historic sites and buildings, Mountain View can continue its urban evolution while retaining a unique sense of place over 160 years in the making.

CHAPTER 1

THE LOST OLD TOWN
EARLY EL CAMINO REAL

Picket fences line El Camino Real in this bird's-eye view of Mountain View's first high school (left), built in 1902, and second grammar school building, built in 1872. The schools were located in the town of Old Mountain View, centered near El Camino Real and Highway 237. This chapter uncovers this long-lost town's hidden history. (Courtesy MVHA.)

The Taylor Hotel was an Old Mountain View landmark located on the site of the town's first stagecoach stop. Originally built by William Elliot, it was purchased by Samuel and Leticia Taylor in 1861. The building offered 15 boarding rooms and a large social hall, home to fraternal meetings and religious services. The hotel burned down in 1911, and today, the site is a BMW dealership. A marker commemorating the town of Old Mountain View was placed here in 1979. (Historical image courtesy MVHA.)

THE LOST OLD TOWN: EARLY EL CAMINO REAL

Two tall palm trees still mark the location of the Taylor family house at 96 West El Camino Real. The 1877 Victorian home pictured above was an Old Mountain View landmark until it was demolished in 1960 to make way for the Cusimano Family Colonial Mortuary. In addition to running their mortuary, Joseph and Sue Cusimano were active participants in Mountain View's civic life. Joseph served on the city council from 1968 to 1974 and as mayor in 1974. (Historical image courtesy MVHA.)

The Whelan blacksmith shop was an Old Mountain View landmark from 1863 until 1945. Irish immigrants Daniel and Margaret Whelan operated the shop and raised their family in Old Mountain View. Their son, Charles Whelan, took over operations and rebuilt the blacksmith shop after the 1860 structure seen above burned down in 1911. The intersection of Highway 237 and El Camino Real now covers this historic site. (Historical image courtesy MVHA.)

A tire shop and El Camino Real's intersection with Highway 237 now occupy the site of blacksmith Charles Whelan's simple Victorian home, pictured below. The home was located just up the road from the family's blacksmith shop. Whelan resided in this house until his death in 1960. (Historical image courtesy MVHA.)

El Camino Real's 1898 bridge over Stevens Creek is featured on the historic postcard below. The creek's running water and shaded banks created a natural resting spot for Gold Rush–era travelers on the old highway, likely leading to Mountain View's establishment as a stagecoach stop. Today, the creek can be enjoyed via the popular Stevens Creek Trail. Construction on the trail began in 1991 at Shoreline Park and was extended to this location in 2009. (Historical image courtesy Kevin Duggan.)

THE LOST OLD TOWN: EARLY EL CAMINO REAL

St. Joseph's Catholic Church was founded as a satellite mission of the Santa Clara Mission Church in 1867. The simple white structure was built near Stevens Creek on land donated by San Franciscan John Sullivan. The church relocated to its present site in New Mountain View in 1905. Today, the original site on the northeast corner of Mountain View–Alviso Road (now Yuba Drive) and El Camino Real is occupied by a car dealership. (Historical image courtesy MVHA.)

THE LOST OLD TOWN: EARLY EL CAMINO REAL

The town of Old Mountain View was well served by a number of drinking establishments. One of the earliest was the Farmers Exchange Saloon, owned by Richard Harjes. Harjes was a German immigrant who came to Mountain View in 1868. His home (left) and saloon (middle) are seen in this early photograph of El Camino Real near Bay Street. Today, the site, at 64 West El Camino Real, is occupied by the Hotel Lodge. (Historical image courtesy MVHA.)

THE LOST OLD TOWN: EARLY EL CAMINO REAL

Old Mountain View and New Mountain View were viewed as two separate settlements when brothers Victor and Andrew Manfredi emigrated from Palermo, Italy, in the 1880s. Victor opened a general store on El Camino Real, pictured below, and came to be known as the "Mayor of Old Mountain View." Today, the site of his store is occupied by an In-N-Out Burger restaurant. (Historical image courtesy MVHA.)

The 1981 Two Worlds mixed-use development stands on the site of the Highway Elementary School. Built in 1928 on land formerly occupied by Mountain View's high school and elementary school, the Highway School's El Camino Real location was a reminder that the old highway preceded Castro Street as Mountain View's main civic thoroughfare. The school closed in 1955 and was used from 1958 to 1962 as the first location of Foothill Community College. (Historical image courtesy Kevin Duggan.)

The Lost Old Town: Early El Camino Real

A few vestiges of Old Mountain View still lined El Camino Real at Bay Street when this 1950s photograph was taken. The two-story building at center was Enterprise Hall, an Old Mountain View social hall and commercial building constructed in 1876. The screen of the Monte Vista Drive-In Theatre, visible in the background, foreshadows the historic area's transformation into a car-oriented suburban strip. As the modern image illustrates, these unique landmarks have been replaced by nondescript structures. (Historical image courtesy MVHA.)

THE LOST OLD TOWN: EARLY EL CAMINO REAL

The town of Old Mountain View has been erased from El Camino Real. However, one old town structure survived the bulldozer via relocation. This 1903 image shows the 1875 Dr. Nathaniel Eaton house being transported from El Camino Real to 842 Dana Street. The house was relocated again to 1076 Wright Avenue. Although its second floor was removed in the 1960s, the house survives as the last building from Old Mountain View. (Historical image courtesy MVHA.)

CHAPTER

MOUNTAIN VIEW STATION

CASTRO STREET AND VICINITY

When the railroad bypassed Mountain View in 1864, a new settlement called "Mountain View Station" or "New Mountain View" emerged near the depot. Castro Street, seen here looking south from Villa Street in 1915, became the new community's downtown. This chapter explores the growth of Castro Street and the surrounding neighborhoods—the historic heart of modern Mountain View. (Courtesy MVHA.)

The 1870 Weilheimer Building at 124–126 Castro Street is perhaps the oldest commercial building in northern Santa Clara County still standing. Restoration was initiated in 2006 by former owner Terry Kline. The building was originally constructed by brothers Samuel and Seligman Weilheimer, Jewish emigrants from Germany, as the Mountain View Station branch of their Old Mountain View general store. Seligman's son, Julius, took over operations and lived nearby at 938 Villa Street, which is now Chez TJ restaurant. (Historical image courtesy MVHA.)

MOUNTAIN VIEW STATION: CASTRO STREET AND VICINITY

In 1888, Mountain View welcomed the completion of a new Southern Pacific train depot. Previously, a variety of structures served as depots, including a converted saloon. The second floor of the new depot was used as a residence for the local station agent. In 1959, the depot was considered out of date and was unceremoniously replaced with a cement block waiting shelter. In 2002, the city corrected that mistake by constructing a replica of the depot about 500 feet closer to Castro Street at Centennial Plaza. (Historical image courtesy MVHA.)

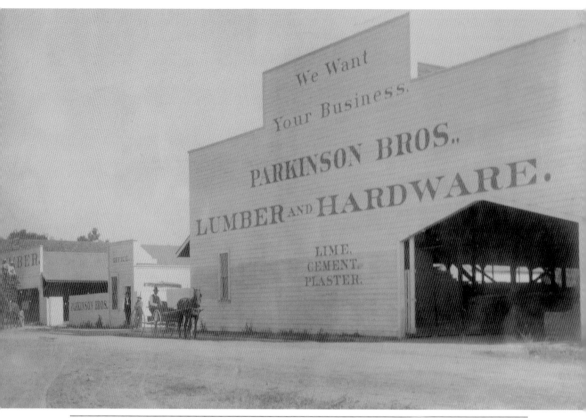

Built in 1897, the Parkinson Brothers Lumber and Hardware Company plant was on Front Street (now Evelyn Avenue) between View and Bush Streets. In 1911, the business was purchased by Earl D. Minton and renamed the Minton Lumber Company. The company helped fuel the growth of early Mountain View. The original plant site was developed as housing in 1996. In 2010, after 99 years in business, Minton Lumber Company ceased operations at 455 West Evelyn Avenue. (Historical image courtesy MVHA.)

MOUNTAIN VIEW STATION: CASTRO STREET AND VICINITY

The southeast corner of Villa and Hope Streets is currently home to the Mountain View Post Office. In the early 1900s, it was the location of Daniel Marcus Farr's carriage and machinery shop. The shop's simple wooden building, pictured below, was typical of early commercial structures in the city. After many years operating out of Castro Street storefronts, the post office constructed a building here in 1960. It was replaced in 2002 with the current structure. (Historical image courtesy MVHA.)

Chinese immigrant Yuen Lung came to Mountain View in 1879 and opened the store pictured below on the northwest corner of Villa and View Streets. Over time, Chinese- and Japanese-owned businesses concentrated around his store, and the area became known as Mountain View's Chinatown. Upon his death in 1932, the *San Jose Evening News* described Lung as a "noted citizen, respected by all races and creeds" and "Mountain View's Chinese Patriarch." Most of Chinatown burned down in 1946. (Historical image courtesy MVPL.)

Typical Suburban Home—Mountain View, California

The 1897 home on the corner of Villa and Oak Streets is one of Mountain View's largest examples of Queen Anne Victorian architecture. It was built for Judge Benjamin E. Burns and his wife, Katherine Henley Burns. Judge Burns served as the city's second mayor from 1904 to 1906 and again from 1909 to 1910. The home was later converted to apartments, and much of its Victorian detailing was removed. It was extensively remodeled in 2011–2012. (Historical image courtesy Kevin Duggan.)

When the above image was taken in 1900, the intersection of California Street and Mariposa Avenue was Mountain View's countryside. Houses were built at 1610 California Street (left, under construction) and 1560 California Street for those who wanted to live on larger lots outside of town. The countryside is gone now, but both homes still stand. The 1560 California Street address is notable for being the first location of Mountain View's Community School of Music and Arts (Historical image courtesy MVHA.)

In 1904, the relocation of the Oakland-based Pacific Press Publishing Company transformed Mountain View. The Seventh-Day Adventist—owned company became Mountain View's first major industry and brought approximately 100 Adventist families to town. The building featured here served as company headquarters from 1907 until 1983, when the Pacific Press relocated to Idaho. In 2011, the campus at 1200 Villa Street was purchased by Google, thus restoring its status as home to Mountain View's largest employer. (Historical image courtesy MVHA.)

From 1907 to 1971, Mountain View's Seventh-Day Adventist church stood on the corner of Bailey Avenue (now Shoreline Boulevard) and West Dana Street. The church served the large Pacific Press Adventist community. In 1967, a new church was built on Springer Road in Los Altos. The church "returned" to Mountain View by asking the two cities to slightly adjust their shared borders. Today, the original site is home to Mountain View Academy, an Adventist high school. (Historical image courtesy MVHA.)

MOUNTAIN VIEW STATION: CASTRO STREET AND VICINITY

The oak-shaded lot that is now home to Mariposa Park was previously occupied by a collection of residential structures partially pictured in this image taken from West Dana Street. The two-story structure on the left was built in 1910 as a barn. The surrounding cottages were built in the 1930s and 1940s by Bernard and Lela Rasmussen, an Adventist couple, to house their Rasmussen School of Craft. The site was cleared in 2011 for Mariposa Park's construction. (Historical image by author.)

The house at 336 Mariposa Avenue was built in 1908 for Wilbur Lee Camp and his wife, Elizabeth Burns Camp. Wilbur Camp, a veteran of the Spanish-American War in the Philippines, moved to California in 1905 and helped organize the Farmers and Merchants Bank. He retired in 1940 as the manager of the bank, which by then was a branch of Bank of America. (Historical image courtesy MVHA.)

The historic sandstone building at 201 Castro Street was built in 1905 for the Farmers and Merchants Bank. The bank was organized by a group of local men led by Jacob Mockbee and Wilbur Camp, who served as its first president and cashier, respectively. In 1927, it became a branch of the Bank of Italy, the predecessor to Bank of America. Since 1990, it has been home to the Red Rock Coffee House. (Historical image courtesy MVHA.)

Broken windows and rubble are visible on the ground floor of the April 1906 photograph of the Ames Building below, taken shortly after the Great San Francisco Earthquake shook down the building's rear wall. The structure was built in 1903 by Prof. Daniel T. Ames, a nationally renowned handwriting expert. In 2003, owners Al and Audrey Jehning restored the building's facade. It now stands proudly as one of downtown's most handsome historic landmarks. (Historical image courtesy MVHA.)

In 1894, Thomas Rogers and his nephew, Arthur Rogers, opened the Rogers and Rogers General Store on Castro Street. The current building, at 142–156 Castro Street, was constructed by Rogers and Rogers after the 1906 earthquake destroyed their original structure. Mountain View's post office was located here until 1928. The second floor was home to the Mountain View Hotel. Over the years, facade alterations have obscured the building's age; the current facade is from 2005. (Historical image courtesy MVHA.)

The Mockbee Building was constructed in 1906 by Jacob Mockbee, an early town trustee, mayor (1916–1918), and reported descendant of Daniel Boone. Until 1962, its first floor was home to a hardware store. From 1984 to 2012, the building was home to Kapp's Pizza Bar and Grill. Owned by brothers Joe and Larry Kapp, the restaurant was decorated with sports memorabilia reflecting Joe Kapp's legendary career as a University of California quarterback and football coach. (Historical image courtesy MVHA.)

Although Mountain View incorporated as a city on November 7, 1902, the town's first official city hall building, pictured below, was not constructed until 1909. The two-story Mission Revival–style structure on the southeast corner of California and Castro Streets housed government offices, the police station, the jail, and the library. City offices outgrew the building in 1959, and it was demolished in 1962. A bank was built, which later became a restaurant. The current building was constructed in 2002. (Historical image courtesy MVHA.)

In 1913, the First National Bank built an imposing Neoclassical-style structure on the southwest corner of Castro and Villa Streets. The pediment and four large columns visible in the historical postcard below were stripped away in the 1950s.

In 1970, the building was purchased by the Independent Order of Odd Fellows (IOOF). IOOF's Mountain View chapter, established in 1876, still occupies the building today. (Historical image courtesy Jim Hickman.)

MOUNTAIN VIEW STATION: CASTRO STREET AND VICINITY

In 1926, after 16 years of bringing Hollywood to Mountain View at the Glen Theatre at 174 Castro Street, Fritz Campen opened the Mountain View Theatre at 228 Castro Street. Designed by noted theater architect Alexander Cantin, the *Mountain View Register-Leader* declared of it, "There will not be another show house on the peninsula with a more beautiful facade, and few if any with a more commodious or more comfortable interior." The heavily altered building is now a nightclub. (Historical image courtesy MVPL.)

In 1915, the California Supply Company opened a pickle factory on the corner of Franklin and Villa Streets. The pungent plant was a local landmark until its 1963 demolition. Mountain View Water Works operated the water tower visible in the background. By 1980, the block was cleared for construction of the current Police and Fire Administration Building. The building was renamed in 2004 to honor former police chief and mayor Robert K. Schatz. (Historical image courtesy MVPL.)

MOUNTAIN VIEW STATION: CASTRO STREET AND VICINITY

Mountain View's Fire Station 1, pictured above, and the adjacent Dana Street Park were built in 1994 on the former site of Dana Street School. Built in 1916, Dana Street School was the city's second public elementary school and the first in New Mountain View. The school was closed in 1959 after being declared seismically unsafe in 1955. Students relocated to the new Edith Landels Elementary School, named after a longtime Dana Street School kindergarten teacher. (Historical image courtesy MVHA.)

Pioneer Memorial Park's name is appropriate, as some of Mountain View's pioneers still rest in peace below its rolling lawns. In 1861, Maria Castro donated the land to the Presbyterian church for the creation of the nondenominational Mountain View Cemetery. Burials ceased in 1905, and in 1930, the city took ownership. During park construction in 1966, unclaimed remains and tombstones were buried in place. "Memorial" was added back to the park's name during a rededication in 2000. (Historical image courtesy MVHA.)

Mountain View's Masonic Temple, at 890 Church Street, was originally built in 1932 as the American Legion Memorial Hall. In 1936, the building went up for sale via a mortgage foreclosure and was purchased by the local Masons. Mountain View's Masonic Lodge No. 194 was founded in 1868, just down the street in the second floor of the Presbyterian church, where Wells Fargo bank now stands. (Courtesy MVHA.)

MOUNTAIN VIEW STATION: CASTRO STREET AND VICINITY

Few lost landmarks are as fondly remembered as the 1924 Mountain View Union High School. After extensive debate, the school was closed in 1981 due to declining enrollment, limited expansion options, and the desire to increase student diversity at Awalt (now Mountain View) and Los Altos High Schools. The sturdy edifice went down fighting; the wrecking ball bounced off its walls during demolition in 1987. A few salvaged architectural elements from the structure were incorporated into the existing Park Place mixed-use development. (Historical image courtesy MVPL.)

MOUNTAIN VIEW STATION: CASTRO STREET AND VICINITY

Today's Eagle Park was once the home field for generations of Mountain View High Eagles. The historical image below depicts the football field, named in 1961 after longtime coach Wendell Grubb, when it featured lights and stands salvaged in 1940 from the San Francisco World's Fair on Treasure Island. Football games were big community events, especially in 1975, when the underdog "Miracle of Mountain View" team won Mountain View High's only division championship to date. (Historical image courtesy Eugene Sharp.)

The author's grandmother Emma
Sias is pictured visiting downtown
Mountain View for the first time
with her friend Enedina Jones in
1948. Behind them stands Veglia's
Department Store, originally built
in 1908 as Scarpa's Meat Market
and today home to Seascapes
Fish and Pets. In the modern
photograph, Sias enjoys a trip
downtown with her daughter
Gloria Perry (the author's mother).
Although businesses and buildings
have come and gone, Castro
Street remains the vibrant heart of
Mountain View. (Historical image
courtesy Emma Sias.)

CHAPTER 3

VALLEY OF HEART'S DELIGHT
MOUNTAIN VIEW'S COUNTRYSIDE

An apricot-cutting party is shown in this 1896 photograph of the area now occupied by San Antonio Shopping Center. Santa Clara Valley was once known as the Valley of Heart's Delight due to its agricultural prosperity. This chapter reveals the lost rural landscape surrounding Mountain View during its first century. (Courtesy Wallace Erichsen and Ruth Job Erichsen.)

The first permanent residence in what is now Mountain View was built in 1842 by Francisco Estrada near today's Central Expressway and Rengstorff Avenue. Estrada's adobe was the focal point of the vast Rancho Pastoría de las Borregas. After his death in 1845, ownership transferred to Estrada's father-in-law, Mariano Castro. Castro built the residence shown above in 1850. The site's existing strip mall is notable for housing the original location of the local restaurant chain Hobee's, which opened in 1974. (Historical image courtesy MVHA.)

VALLEY OF HEART'S DELIGHT: MOUNTAIN VIEW'S COUNTRYSIDE

In 1911, Mariano Castro's youngest son, Crisanto, built a new home named Villa Francesca in honor of his late wife, Francesca. The Castro family lived in Villa Francesca until 1958, when his daughter, Mercedes Castro, sold the villa and surrounding lands to the city for the establishment of a museum and park. The villa was demolished in 1961 after being partially damaged by a suspicious fire. Today, the site is occupied by Rengstorff Park's picnic grounds. (Historical image courtesy MVPL.)

Matt Pear, a former councilmember and the mayor of Mountain View in 2004, is seen here in 2012 and 1965 standing with his brother Mark (right) on the site of their family's Ortega Avenue cherry orchard. Their grandparents, Martin and Milica Pear, established their family's ranch in the late 1800s after emigrating from Croatia. The Pear family ranch was one of many in the immediate vicinity to be developed as high-density housing in the 1960 and 1970s. (Both images courtesy Edna Pear.)

VALLEY OF HEART'S DELIGHT: MOUNTAIN VIEW'S COUNTRYSIDE

At the end of Prohibition, John Gemello and his son, Mario, opened the Gemello Winery on the family's 55-acre fruit orchard at 2003 West El Camino Real. The historical image shows the winery's El Camino Real sign in 1955, before the Camino Bowl was built in front of the winery. From 1934 to 1982, the winery bottled locally grown grapes, mostly from vineyards in the Santa Cruz Mountains. Today, the Gemello Village development occupies the site. (Historical image courtesy Katherine Gemello.)

Mountain View's Japanese and Portuguese communities have a deep history in the former agricultural lands along Stierlin Road, as exemplified in this photographic pairing. The historical image shows the ranch of Japanese immigrants Shuichi and Asa Hori, while the modern photograph shows the Irmandade da Festa do Espírito (IFES) hall built on the same site in 1931. IFES was founded in 1926 by Portuguese dairymen and shares its origins with the Sociedade da Festa Velha do Divino Espírito Santo (SFV) on Villa Street. (Historical image courtesy MVHA.)

Until the 1950s, the area now known as the Cuesta Park neighborhood was a seemingly endless expanse of fruit orchards. A vast portion of the neighborhood was owned by local pioneer Benjamin T. Bubb, for whom Bubb Elementary School is named. The Bubb family home, pictured below, was near the corner of today's Leona Lane and Begen Avenue. In 1959, the site was developed as the new location of Mountain View's First Presbyterian Church. (Historic photograph courtesy MVHA.)

The Craftsman farmhouse pictured below was built in 1909 by orchardists Barney and Juliette Job. In its later years, the home was a hidden landmark, set back from Grant Road and surrounded by trees. From 1987 to 2006, the Schmitz family tended Mountain View's last farm on a 15-acre property surrounding the home. Their beloved farm, locally known as the "pumpkin patch," was cleared for a subdivision, The Enclave at Waverly Park, in 2010. (Historical image courtesy Wallace Erichsen and Ruth Job Erichsen.)

Barney and Juliette Job's son Merle Job lived across Grant Road from his parents' orchard in this modest home with his wife, Alpha, and their children, Thomas and Ruth. Here, baby Thomas sits in a high chair near the family's orchard. In 1989, the El Camino YMCA opened on the site. Oaks and ornamental cherry trees surround the YMCA, paying homage to the site's historic landscape. (Historical image courtesy Wallace Erichsen and Ruth Job Erichsen.)

VALLEY OF HEART'S DELIGHT: MOUNTAIN VIEW'S COUNTRYSIDE

Joseph Eastwood Sr. built this Spanish-style home in his orchard at 1885 Miramonte Avenue in 1919. Since 1955, the campus of St. Francis High School has grown around the historic residence, now known as the Andre House and used for school offices. The school's oldest landmark, however, is its massive California bay tree, visible below to the left of the house. The tree grows within Ron Calcagno Stadium, home to the St. Francis Lancers' popular Friday night football games. (Historical image courtesy St. Francis High School.)

VALLEY OF HEART'S DELIGHT: MOUNTAIN VIEW'S COUNTRYSIDE

The Minton Company built this large Tudor-style home at 1855 Miramonte Avenue for William Patrick Wright and his wife, Nellie Swall Wright, in 1927 in what was then Mountain View's countryside. William Wright was a real estate broker and founder of Mountain View's First National Bank. Since 1965, the property has been the location of the Villa Siena senior living community. In 2009, the house was relocated on-site to make way for a complete reconstruction of the facility. The modern photograph above shows the home undergoing restoration. (Historical image courtesy Honor Spitz.)

VALLEY OF HEART'S DELIGHT: MOUNTAIN VIEW'S COUNTRYSIDE

Dating back to 1868, El Monte Avenue is one of Mountain View's oldest streets. The area near El Monte's intersection with El Camino Real was once known as the Junction. Built in 1906 by Victor Anzini, the Junction House (pictured below) was the Junction's most visible landmark until fire consumed it in 1941. The Junction House served many roles: country inn, social hall, picnic ground, and Prohibition-era speakeasy. Today, the site is occupied by Office Depot. (Historical image courtesy MVHA.)

Charles Skinner built the Junction Garage opposite the Junction House in 1912. The garage is shown above after its expansion in 1917. It was purchased by Emil Schmidt in 1919. The garage fronted a short stretch of El Camino Real that once jogged sharply to the north at El Monte Avenue. After El Camino Real's route was smoothed, the jog became an extension of El Monte, and the garage site became a median. (Historical image courtesy Carol Rudgers.)

El Camino Real's transition from country highway to suburban strip is captured in this 1950s photograph, taken in front of Bolster TV Repair at 1962 West El Camino Real. The tiled arch on the right once led to the Mission Rabbitry, a 1920s rabbit farm listed in early advertisements as being "North of Junction" and offering "Rabbits: For Food, Fur, & Fancy." The rabbitry arch and television repair shop were replaced by a Sizzler in 1971. (Historical image courtesy Peggy Bolster Crowder.)

VALLEY OF HEART'S DELIGHT: MOUNTAIN VIEW'S COUNTRYSIDE

4

MID-CENTURY
MOUNTAIN VIEW
LANDMARKS OF THE
POSTWAR BOOM

Rex Gobolic opened the Camino Bowl at 2025 West El Camino Real in 1956 on land leased from the Gemello family in front of their winery. The alley closed in 1996, when it was replaced by the Gemello Village development. This chapter focuses on mid-century landmarks like the Camino Bowl that modernized Mountain View during the postwar boom. (Courtesy MVPL.)

Ferry-Morse Seed Company was the last major agriculture-related industry to open in Mountain View. In 1951, the company relocated its western headquarters to the corner of Evelyn Avenue and Whisman Road. Mountain View's rapid urbanization prompted Ferry-Morse to relocate to Modesto in 1985. The building was demolished and replaced by the Mountain View Corporate Center office park. The adjacent portion of Whisman Road's original right-of-way is named Ferry-Morse Way. (Historical image courtesy MVPL.)

MID-CENTURY MOUNTAIN VIEW: LANDMARKS OF THE POSTWAR BOOM

In 1953, Sylvania Electronic Defense Laboratory opened at 123 Whisman Road, just down the street from Ferry-Morse Seed Company. The two neighboring corporations were good representatives of Mountain View's transition in the 1950s, with one foot in an agricultural past and the other in a high-tech future. Sylvania merged with GTE in 1959 and became one of Mountain View's largest employers. In 1999, the site of more than 50 acres became Whisman Station, a neighborhood centered on a new light-rail line. (Historical image courtesy of the author.)

In 1957, eight employees left Shockley Semiconductor at 391 San Antonio Road, the Silicon Valley's first silicon-based lab, to form Fairchild Semiconductor, arguably the valley's first successful startup. Known today in high-tech lore as the "traitorous eight," their company expanded rapidly and fueled Silicon Valley's early growth. In 1958, Fairchild Semiconductor's headquarters, seen here, were constructed at 545 Whisman Road. Today, the site is occupied by offices for the Internet security company Symantec. (Courtesy Mountain View History Center.)

Walker's Wagon Wheel was a popular hangout for Fairchild employees and other workers in Mountain View's first major high-tech industrial district along Whisman Road. Deals were made and ideas were exchanged over food and drink at the popular Western-themed restaurant. A card room was added in 1995, but the permit was revoked in 1999, leading to the restaurant's closure in 2000. The abandoned building at 282 East Middlefield Road was demolished in 2003. (Courtesy Mountain View History Center.)

In 1934, during the Great Depression's peak, Mountain View's junior chamber of commerce raised funds for a community center on Moffett Boulevard. Adobe bricks made on-site by government work-welfare laborers lent the structure its name, the Adobe Building. In 1959, the porch was enclosed, as seen below. The Mountain View Historical Association's "Save the Adobe" campaign halted demolition in 1995. The Adobe was seismically retrofitted and restored in 2001 and is now listed on the National Register of Historic Places. (Historical image courtesy MVHA.)

Days before Disneyland opened, the front page of the *Mountain View Register-Leader* featured the park's Casey Junior train peering out the door of 243 Moffett Boulevard. The 1946 structure, a potential candidate for the National Register of Historic Places, was the first home of Arrow Development, the company that manufactured many of Disneyland's original attractions. After engineering Disneyland's Matterhorn, the first modern steal-tube roller coaster, Arrow relocated to 1555 Plymouth Street, where it remained until 1984. (Historical image courtesy MVHA.)

Lane's opened in 1947 as the self-proclaimed "most beautiful drive-in on El Camino Real." The circular building was described in a 1946 issue of *Architectural Record* as combining "the processes of ice-cream manufacturing with the principles of drive-in distribution." In 1948, Lane's became Johnny Mac's, a popular teenager hangout where carhops served "Big Mac" burgers long before McDonald's did so. The building still stands today, perhaps awaiting a tenant that will restore the glamour of its postwar heyday. (Historical image courtesy MVHA.)

Mancini Motors was on the southeast corner of El Camino Real and Castro Street from 1940 to 1974. Visible in the historical nighttime image below is the dealership's five-story tower topped by a rotating globe that owner Ugo Mancini salvaged from the 1939 Treasure Island World's Fair's Chrysler Exhibit. After the dealership relocated to Sunnyvale, the site was cleared for the existing bank building, which features a mosaic depicting Mountain View's history. Ugo Mancini's 1950 Moderne-style home still stands at 334 Church Street. (Historical image courtesy MVPL.)

When Sears opened in 1957, it signaled the rise of San Antonio Road as Mountain View's new commercial center. Sears was one of the earliest retailers to opt for a suburban location over downtown Mountain View. By the 1990s, the trend reversed, as malls like San Antonio Center became outdated and Castro Street revitalized. The modern image above shows Sears in 2011, as it was being demolished to create a downtown-like mix of stores, restaurants, and housing. (Historical image courtesy MVPL.)

MID-CENTURY MOUNTAIN VIEW: LANDMARKS OF THE POSTWAR BOOM

After 26 years on Castro Street, J.C. Penney left downtown to become the anchor tenant of the new Mayfield Mall on San Antonio Road, pictured here. Built in 1966, the indoor mall was the first of its kind locally. Competition from larger malls prompted closure in 1983 and conversion into offices for Hewlett Packard, which remained until 2003. Plans for residential redevelopment were shelved in 2012 in favor of renovating the former mall for new office tenants. (Historical image by Joe Melena, Courtesy MVPL.)

The Old Mill Specialty Center was a unique indoor mall centered on a tree-lined, koi-filled stream with a custom-built mill wheel. The mall opened in 1975 on California Street, across from San Antonio Center. Designed without an anchor retail tenant, its smaller stores floundered. In 1988, an unsuccessful conversion into a public market removed the mall's award-winning interior. In 1994, the site was razed to build the Crossings, a "new urbanist" neighborhood designed by Calthorpe Associates. (Historical image courtesy MVPL.)

As stores abandoned downtown, city leaders crafted ambitious redevelopment plans. Visions of a skyline filled with high-rises never came to fruition, with one exception: the 12-story tower at 444 Castro Street. Its unique top-down, delay-plagued construction (visible below) made for a bizarre spectacle in the 1970s. Upon its completion in 1981, it stood unoccupied except for security dogs on the ground floor, earning it the nickname Dog City. Now known as Mountain Bay Plaza, the remodeled tower remains the tallest building in town. (Historical image courtesy MVPL.)

As Mountain View expanded in the 1950s, city government quickly outgrew the original 1909 city hall. To free up space, the library relocated from the building's second floor to a storefront at 939 Dana Street. In 1958, the city built a new home for the library on Franklin Street, seen below. The original building was expanded in 1966 into a two-story structure that stood on the site until the current library was built in 1997. (Historical image courtesy MVPL.)

In 1959, the First Presbyterian Church joined the trend of the time and left downtown for a suburban location on Miramonte Avenue. The church's eight-year-old sanctuary on Castro Street was converted into Mountain View's city hall in 1961, as seen above. During renovation in 1984, structural deficiencies were so severe that the building was demolished. In 1991, a new $44.5-million civic center was completed as the centerpiece of Castro Street's revitalization. The tree visible in both images is the focal point of the city's holiday tree lighting. (Historical image courtesy MVPL.)

MID-CENTURY MOUNTAIN VIEW: LANDMARKS OF THE POSTWAR BOOM

Meryvn's Fine Foods was one of the last old-fashioned American diners on Castro Street. The restaurant opened next-door to the Mountain View Theatre in the 1960s. Although the restaurant closed in the 1990s, its back lounge remains in operation as a small, unsigned bar accessed from a side alley. The recent addition of a pseudo-historic facade obscures the building's mid-century origins. (Historical image courtesy Mountain View History Center.)

Multistory downtown office buildings with upscale restaurants on the ground floor now dominate the intersection of Castro and California Streets. The building at 383 Castro Street is a reminder of a time when one-story buildings and parking lots gave the intersection a more suburban feel. Until 2003, the building was home to Der Wienerschnitzel. The hot dog chain's original 1968 A-frame building was a popular hangout for students from nearby Mountain View Union High School. (Courtesy Mountain View History Center.)

When Linda's Drive-In closed in 1985, the *San Jose Mercury News* eulogized the diner as "the stuff of teenage dreams." Dean and Rebecca Riggs opened the drive-in on El Camino Real at Escuela Avenue in 1956. Diners devoured its legendary Parisian burgers, smothered in secret sauce between buns from the Parisian Bakery. To the delight of Parisian-craving locals, Armadillo Willy's in Los Altos began serving the burger in 2009. The Wolf Camera store that replaced Linda's closed in July 2012. (Historical image courtesy Mountain View History Center.)

LINDA'S

The finest in service and the best hamburgers for over 25 years. Located on the corner of El Camino and Escuela.

City leaders initially hesitated to approve construction of the Emporium on El Camino Real at Highway 85, far from the San Antonio Road retail zone. But by 1970, the San Francisco-based department store was open for business on the former Dale family ranch. Locals mourned its closure in 1995, when the chain was absorbed into Macy's. Voters rejected a contentious proposal for a Home Depot here in 2002. The current building was constructed in 2007 and houses the Palo Alto Medical Foundation's Mountain View Center. (Historical image courtesy MVPL.)

As new single-family-home neighborhoods rapidly replaced the orchards south of El Camino Real in the 1950s, city leaders saw the need for a large new park in the area. A bond was passed in 1966, and Cuesta Park was built on 26 acres of former orchard land along Cuesta Drive. The park's tall redwoods were only saplings when the photograph above was taken, allowing for a clear view of the 1961 tower of El Camino Hospital. (Historical image courtesy Mountain View History Center.)

NORTH BAYSHORE AND MOFFETT FIELD
MOUNTAIN VIEW'S LAST FRONTIER

The North Bayshore district, located between the Bayshore Highway (101) and the San Francisco Bay, was Mountain View's last rural neighborhood. This 1960s aerial photograph shows the district prior to its transformation into a premier Silicon Valley office area. Arrow Development's roller coaster plant is visible to the left of the large Moffett Drive-In Theatre parking lot, which is now Century 16 Theatres. (Courtesy Mountain View History Center.)

German immigrant Henry Rengstorff came to California for the Gold Rush but made his fortune farming and shipping. Rengstorff's Italianate Victorian was built in 1867 on 164 acres of land near his bayside shipping port, known as Rengstorff Landing. The home fell into severe disrepair and was damaged by motorcycle gangs by the late 1970s. The photograph below shows the home in 1980, after the city relocated it from 1737 Stierlin Road (now Shoreline Boulevard) to Shoreline Park. Restoration was completed in 1991. (Historical image courtesy MVHA.)

In 1869, Henry Rengstorff helped establish the Whisman School District for children living near the city's bay lands. The district was named after early settler and stagecoach line operator John W. Whisman. The Whisman School's third edifice is pictured standing on the rural Stierlin Road (now Shoreline Boulevard) in 1961, the same year it relocated to Easy Street. The school closed in 2000, shortly before the Whisman School District merged into the Mountain View-Whisman School District. (Historical image courtesy MVHA.)

Conrad Stierlin immigrated to Mountain View from Switzerland in 1852 and lived in this house, where La Avenida now intersects with Armand Avenue. Stierlin's large Los Alamos ranch included land now occupied by Microsoft and the Santiago Villa mobile home park. Mountain View's historic north-south thoroughfare, Shoreline Boulevard, was named Stierlin Road until 1987. A portion of the road near downtown retains the original name. (Historical image courtesy MVHA.)

In 1863, James and Emily Huff arrived on a wagon train and established a ranch near Charleston Road. The site of their home at 1646 Plymouth Street, near Huff Avenue, is currently occupied by Google offices. In 1950, the *Mountain View Register-Leader* celebrated the home's restoration and speculated, "What its fate is to be in coming years depends upon discernment and vision of whoever takes it over." Sadly, in 1968, motorcycle gangs "took it over" and ravaged the structure. (Historical image courtesy MVHA.)

The Mission Revival campus at the heart of Moffett Field is known as the Shenandoah Plaza National Historic District and was constructed by the US Navy in 1933. Since 1994, it has been managed by NASA, which is transforming the area around the plaza into an education and technology-oriented research campus. NASA's adjacent Ames Research Center was established in 1939. (Historical image courtesy US Navy, via Moffett Field Historical Society.)

For the first time since construction in 1933, the steel skeleton of Hangar One at Moffett Field is exposed, offering an opportunity to recreate this historical image. Originally built to house the Navy's USS *Macon* dirigible, the structure covers eight acres and is large enough for six football fields. As of this writing, the hangar's fate is uncertain—toxic siding was removed but funds for a new skin are undetermined. (Historical image courtesy US Navy, via Moffett Field Historical Society.)

This historical image shows a dredging vessel clearing a channel for Mountain View's last shipping facility, the 1923 South Shore Port. Whisman Road once extended directly to the port and the adjacent Kingsport Plunge, a saltwater recreational pool. The land eventually became part of Moffett Field and is now located within Sunnyvale. Public access to the area was restored in 2010 via a Bay Trail extension around Moffett Field's runways. (Historical image courtesy MVHA.)

A herd of dairy cows and a cowboy amble along the banks of Stevens Creek in the 1966 photograph below. The rural scene in the foreground sharply contrasts with the futuristic research buildings and wind tunnels of the NASA Ames Research Center in the background. The location today looks fairly similar except the cows and cowboy have been replaced by cyclists and joggers enjoying the popular Stevens Creek Trail. (Historical image courtesy Mountain View History Center.)

The landmark tent of Shoreline Amphitheatre was raised in 1986 in a city partnership with Bill Graham Presents. At the time, the tent was the largest of its kind. It was built on a former landfill, and early concertgoers experienced small methane gas fires when cigarettes were put out in its lawn seating area. Methane gas extraction, barriers, and monitoring have since made the lawn a safe place to enjoy concerts. (Historical image by Sam Forencich; courtesy MVPL.)

Over the years, Mountain View has been home to a fair share of computer history milestones and has served as the headquarters of computer-industry game changers like Shockley Laboratories, Fairchild Semiconductor, Adobe Systems, Netscape, and Google. So it is fitting that the Computer History Museum chose the city as its location. The museum is located at 1401 North Shoreline Boulevard in a building originally constructed by Studios Architects as headquarters for Silicon Graphics, Inc., (SGI) in 1994. (Historical image courtesy MVHA.)

Mountain View's leaders long dreamed of an extensive greenbelt along the neglected bay shoreline. To raise the land above sea level, an innovative deal was brokered to use San Francisco's trash as landfill. In 1983, the landfill was transformed into Shoreline at Mountain View, a regional park featuring a sailing lake, a golf course, and restored marshlands. Today, Shoreline Park is Mountain View's crown jewel, a positive example of the city's dramatic evolution over the past 160 years. (Historical image courtesy MVPL.)

NORTH BAYSHORE AND MOFFETT FIELD: MOUNTAIN VIEW'S LAST FRONTIER

This 1992 photograph was taken from Shoreline Park's Vista Slope when it was still an active landfill. The farmland along Amphitheatre Parkway visible here is now occupied by Google's world headquarters and Charleston Park. Today, the top of Vista Slope offers a quiet retreat where one can take in an impressive vista of the city and the timeless mountain views that inspired its name. (Historical image by Joe Melena, courtesy MVPL.)

DISCOVER THOUSANDS OF LOCAL HISTORY BOOKS FEATURING MILLIONS OF VINTAGE IMAGES

Arcadia Publishing, the leading local history publisher in the United States, is committed to making history accessible and meaningful through publishing books that celebrate and preserve the heritage of America's people and places.

Find more books like this at
www.arcadiapublishing.com

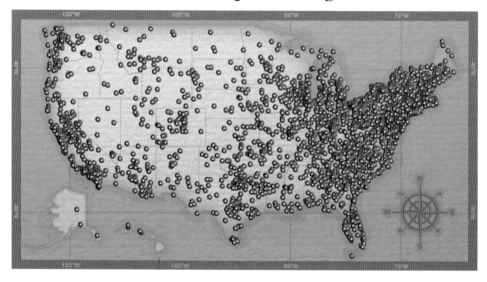

Search for your hometown history, your old stomping grounds, and even your favorite sports team.